I0101753

Author's Guide to Surviving
Self-Publishing

COVERS

E. Gauthier

St. Clair Shores, MI

Hungry Goat Press

www.EATaBOOK.com

Gauthier Publications
P.O. Box 806241
Saint Clair Shores, MI 48080
Attention Permissions Department

Editing: Merideth Hadala
Book Design: Elizabeth Gauthier

This book is non-fiction and should be used for information purposes only.
The material contained does not guarantee results of any kind.
The companies mentioned are in no way affiliated and
are not being promoted.

1st Edition
Hungry Goat Press is an Imprint of Gauthier Publications
www.EATaBOOK.com

ISBN: 978-1-942314-49-3

To all the self-publisher's out there...

You can't judge a book by its cover....

but people do it everyday.

Table of Contents

Books come in four main formats:
1. Hardcover (clothbound)
2. Perfect (soft-cover)
3. ebook (digital)
4. Audio

Introduction

Self-Publishing is a wonderful way to get your book out quickly into the marketplace. While it was once frowned upon, **self-publishing is now a widely used tool that brings authors directly to their audiences.** In fact it is not unheard of for a large publishing house to purchase the rights to the book, repackage it, and sell it under their own branding. As it has evolved, the self-publishing process has gone from standard template books of low quality that screamed self published; to a "sky's the limit" process where an author's vision and creativity can go up against any blockbuster out there. So if you have written a book and are tired of waiting for answers from publishers, or if you are business minded and are excited to do it on your own, then this series is for you. This book is a tool, a short and sweet guide to cover design with a focus on what you need for print and digital publishing. This is a book to read, use and reuse during the publishing process. In the back are workbook pages to help you interview designers, editors, and illustrators. You will also find a handy checklist to make sure you aren't missing a step.

What Makes Up A Book Cover?

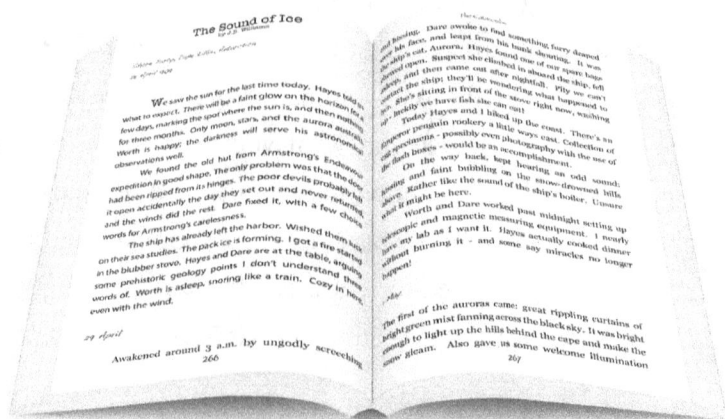

A print book has one file that contains
front, spine and back cover elements.
Turn a book to it side and see how they are a continuous image.

When you say 'cover design' people often think of the front cover of a book. Something eye catching and visually appealing that just screams "buy me!" While a front cover is the most important aspect, if you are printing a book, it is not the only thing you need. Book covers are made of three parts :

1. Front Cover: The front image with title and author.
2. Spine: This is the side of the book you will see if on a bookshelf. This requires the author's name, title and publisher's logo if you have one.
3. Back Cover: The description needs to be here as well as price and a few other things, this will be discussed in greater detail later in the book.

A common misconception people have is what the book cover itself looks like when it goes to print. Even though it has three distinct parts, it is indeed one file. Yes, one file containing three parts. Confused? Don't be, the next section is about templates and it will start to make sense. So go ahead and turn the page.

When you go to print the book you will be asked to give a PDF of the front, spine and back cover all put together...This is because it is printed that way.

Templates

```
                              5.0" X 8.0" Book
                            (127.0mm X 203.2mm)

                                344.0 Page

                                (19.56mm)

                               White Paper




        Barcode
     Location & Size
        2" X 1.2"
```

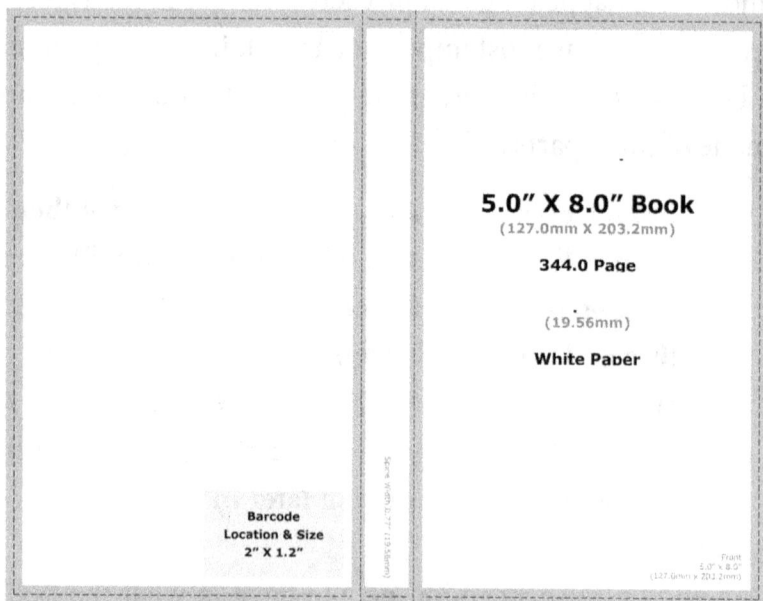

How to read a template:

Main white area or clean areas: This is where your three elements go. The front cover on the right, spine in the middle, and back cover on the left.

Shaded areas around edges: All text and live images need to stay inside the areas. They are a safety zone, so steer clear of them with anything you don't want cut off.

Dashed line: This is where the cover itself will be cut; notice the safety line is before that. This is because machine cuts are not perfect and you don't want a piece of text cut off.

Bleed: : This is where people get confused. You see how the template shaded areas extend out past that cut line? That is the bleed. You must extend your image to the end of the shaded area; the bleed.

You need a few things before you can actually build your template. First and most important is your trim size, how big is your book? There are many standard book sizes from a 6x9 for a fiction title, to an 8x10 for a children's picture book. Go to a bookstore and see what size you prefer. Then you will need the final page count. This includes not only the main interior but the title page, copyright page and any other page inside the book itself. Once you have your page count, you need to decide if you are going to print black and white or full color. Obviously if you have a children's book you are most likely in full color; as opposed to a chapter book that is usually just black and white text. Lastly you will need to decide if your book has a full bleed. An easy way to figure this out is to ask yourself if any of the images extend to the end of your page...Meaning when it's printed, you don't want to see any white along the edges. Picture books are usually full bleed, chapter books often are not, but there are exceptions for both. I will discuss this in more detail in the Interiors book of the series. When you put this information in the template creator, it will create a custom template for you to lay your design over (just like the one on the left). The spine size changes depending on the size of your book, so keep in mind if it is small you might not be able to add text onto it (and that's ok if it's a low page count).

To build your template you need to know:

1. Trim Size
2. Page Count
3. Black and White or Color
4. Full Bleed or No Bleed

Templates are important to have even before you start your design. If you don't start with a template then you are going to have to make your cover fit later...Or hire someone to do it; this can be pricey and avoided. If you look on page 10, this is a basic template. It has the three pieces: the front cover, back cover, and spine all spaced out for you. See those lines, the shaded-in areas that go around the image? Those are your guidelines. That dashed line is the cut line. Every printer and self-publishing platform has a template or a formula to create your cover template. Some of the easiest to use are CreateSpace and Lightning Source. There are many others and, in all honestly, they all contain pretty much the same information. All templates include bleed, cutline, safety zone and of course the bar-code placement. You or your designer need to build the cover on top of the template and keep it as a separate layer. That way you can turn it on and off in whatever program you are using. Once done and everything looks great make sure you save it correctly.

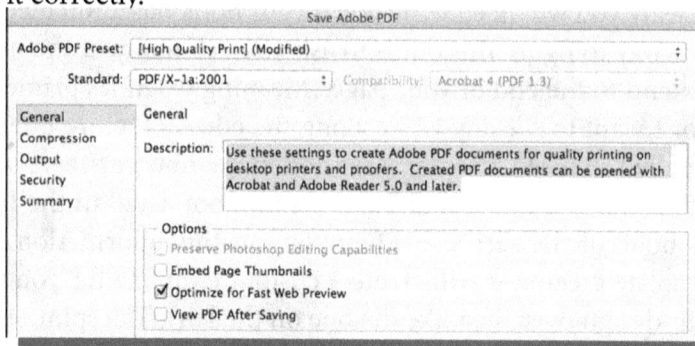

If using Photoshop, go to Save As and select PDF; this will open the menu you see above. Make the settings look like this...See where it says Standard? There's a drop-down menu there; just select the PDF/x-1a:2001 file format. It's the right type of PDF for books.

Always Remember: Turn off the template layer before sending to print or it get printed on the book!

Make sure you send a PDFx-2001 file in CMYK

ISBNs and Barcodes

A n ISBN is very important, but what people don't realize is what they actually mean. Think of an ISBN as a social security number for your book. A unique identifier that belongs to your book and your book alone. It is so unique in fact that each format has its own ISBN. So, if your book is both a perfect-bound (paperback) book and a hardcover edition, you will need two identifiers. **You cannot use the same identifiers for two books!**

An ISBN has 5 parts; often these are separated by commas to make it easier to read.

1. **Prefix element** – This is 978 or 979 currently
2. **Registration group element** – this identifies the particular country, geographical region, or language area participating in the ISBN system. This is between 1 and 5 digits in length.
3. **Registrant element** - this identifies the publisher itself, so if you buy a block of ISBNs these digits will all be the same.
4. **Publication element** – this identifies the edition, it tells you if it's a paperback or hardcover, first edition, second edition etc.
5. **Check digit** – This is the last number and it is actually used by computers to validate. This single digit has a whole crazy math problem behind it!

You do not need to remember all of this but it is nice to know. ISBNs are computer generated...Thank goodness!!!

If you are going through Amazon's KDP platform you do not need a separate ISBN number for your ebook. That being said, as a person in the industry, I still recommend getting one. This is because if you use LSI, IngramSpark, and others you will need a separate ISBN for all formats including ebook. Plus it's a nice little professional looking touch. **Remember you are up against thousands of books; you want to do your best to make yours stand out!**

TIP

If you are buying your own ISBN, you can get it at Bowker - they are a great resource for all things book. The website is ISBN.org. You can also buy your bar-codes here if you need one.

If you are just starting out and on a very tight budget then an alternative to buying your own ISBN for the print version is to go with a service that supplies one for you such as CreateSpace. There are pros and cons to this, so make sure you read the fine print.

Fonts :Is this font ok to use?

Did you know not all fonts are ok to use in books for resale? Many fonts have usage rights and you can get into a lot of trouble if you put them in your book and then sell it. It is very important for this reason that you make sure your fonts are "Free to use commercially." Now one good thing is that standard fonts on a computer are ok to use already, you know the ones that come with Word or Pages or anything that is already listed in a program. This is great because your book interior text is most likely one of these fonts....But maybe not your cover.

Let me stop for a moment and clarify something, I am not tell you to use a standard boring font on cover...In fact I am begging you not to. You just need to make sure that your font is ok to use. How do you check? Simple: If you are using a website like 1001Fonts.com or DaFont.com (great sites by the way) you just have to click the terms listed. It will tell you if it's free to use personally or commercially. Some just say free, some ask that you credit the maker of the font etc. If you already have a working cover you are redesigning or one ready for print, then take a minute and look up your font and see if it's ok to use. If you hire a designer, don't be embarrassed to ask them if they checked, or where the font is from; you don't want to have an issue later.

TIP

Not all fonts work on both Mac and PC; most do but not all. If you have a font downloaded but it doesn't show up on your list, that might be why.

FONTS: Times New Roman
is great but...

There are a ton of fonts out there...Literally thousands; and while you are a bit limited when it comes to the interior of a book (yes it should be easy to read without hurting your eyes), the cover is a whole other animal. If you are hiring the work out (if you have gotten this far in the book you are at least considering it) then your designer should have access to many fonts you have not even heard of. Now let me show you an example:

My Book - Minion Pro

My Book – Amena

MY BOOK – Herculanium

My Book - Blackmoor

My Book – Chalkboard

My Book – Hades

My Book - Orenthal

My Book - Impact

See how the same word can have a different feel depending on the font you use? Happy, silly, serious, creepy... You name it; there is a font for it. When you have your designer do a mock-up, tell them what kind of font you are imagining so they have a good jumping off point.

Images

Images and illustrations can make or break a cover, so it's tempting to just do a Google search of what you are looking for and put the title and your name on it. Unfortunately, 9 times out of 10, you will be knee deep in a copyright issue. Someone took the time to make the image, let's have some respect and give them the credit they deserve. This brings me to my first point: if you love an image, then contact the creator and ask if you can use it in exchange for credit in the book. For some artists, building a portfolio credit is enough; however most people will want to be paid. If you have an image or drawing created, make sure you have the artist sign off on it. I mean an actual piece of paper that you can hold in your hand and put into a folder. If you do it by email, have them sign and email back and print it out. I know it sounds old fashioned but computers break and emails crash: **print it**. You can look online for sample Work for Hire agreements. There are many and you should tailor it as needed.

TIP

There are many sites that have free usage images, you just need to read the fine print and make sure its completely free use. One great example is Pixabay.com

One thing to consider is a custom image. Custom images are great because they are unique to your book and help it to stand out. If you are having an image created, then develop a very clear cut time-line for drafts and a final deadline. If your image is basic, then it might only take a day or two. If it's a hand drawn cover of a specific scene from your book, it will understandably take longer. Always give yourself a few extra days for changes. It is very common for a book cover to have an issue once it is sent to print. Some of the most common errors are:

- Not in CMYK color mode
- Missing bleed
- Live text is to close to safety line
- Front and back cover submitted separately instead of one file.
- Submitted as a jpeg instead of PDF
- Missing spine

TIP

Give yourself at least an additional four days for cover review. You want to make sure your files look good and so does your printer, so make any changes they suggest.

If anything is flagged, you or the designer need to fix it. Most printers will explain what is wrong and most likely it is described in this book. Depending on the problem, it will take time to fix, then resubmit and review. If you have a book launch or an event, having your book done on time is vital. A good rule of thumb is 4 days to a week bumper. I have seen books get approved in 24 hours and some that drag on a month for redesign or formatting issues. If you use this book as a tool then you should get through it in a reasonable time. If you are having trouble, don't worry it will get easier!

Remember a good designer will ask you for the template or a page count and trim size, so they can build the cover correctly from the beginning. Starting out with a template will prevent many issues and get your book to print faster. After all, there is no better feeling than holding your book in your hands for the first time!

Pre-flight

InDesign is the most common (and in my opinion best) tool for book interiors. Some designers also layout the cover in this program. If your designer is using InDesign make sure they do a pre-flight before they export the file. If you are saying "Wait what?" just ask them to preform a pre-flight and send you a screen shot. It is basically a computer generated checklist that will say if any images are low resolution. It will check to make sure fonts are embedded, that everything is CMYK and all kinds of little helpful items. I will go into much more detail about this program in the book on interiors; but for covers, this is all you really need to know. A sample of what a preflight panel looks like is below.

See the little yellow caution sign...It means something has to be fixed...Better have the designer fix it now than have the printer send it back to you to fix later.

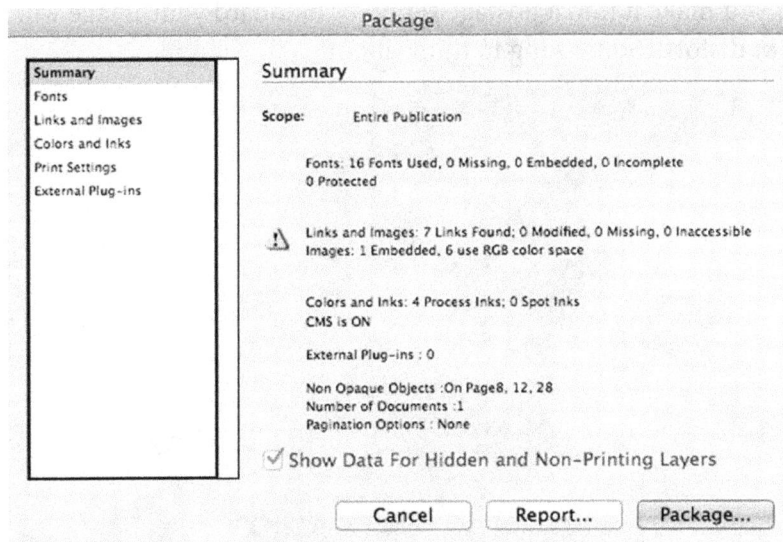

```
                            Package

  Summary           Summary
  Fonts
  Links and Images   Scope:      Entire Publication
  Colors and Inks
  Print Settings              Fonts: 16 Fonts Used, 0 Missing, 0 Embedded, 0 Incomplete
  External Plug-ins           0 Protected

                    ⚠  Links and Images: 7 Links Found; 0 Modified, 0 Missing, 0 Inaccessible
                       Images: 1 Embedded, 6 use RGB color space

                       Colors and Inks: 4 Process Inks; 0 Spot Inks
                       CMS is ON

                       External Plug-ins : 0

                       Non Opaque Objects :On Page8, 12, 28
                       Number of Documents :1
                       Pagination Options : None

                 ✓ Show Data For Hidden and Non-Printing Layers

                        [ Cancel ]   [ Report... ]   [ Package... ]
```

Vector

You might hear the word vector floating around a great deal in the design world. What is it? Well, to best explain it (and keep it short) I will use this example. You take a picture with your camera and make it much bigger....You know how the edges get blurry and pixelated?....Not a vector image. If you take a beautiful piece of vector line art and do the same, it will look identical.

Adobe Illustrator is often used to make vector images. The file name will often end in .EPS or .AI. You may be asking yourself, do I need a vector image for my cover? No, a high resolution image will do just fine. If you end up having a logo created for your publishing company, however, then make sure it's vector. You want to be sure you can print sizes from business card to signs and all things in between.

A Vector image can be sized indefinitely and will not lose quality. If you make it into a postage stamp or billboard your image will not distort...Something to think about!

What is a Wrap cover?

I am a big fan of wrap covers lately, but I will also be the first to admit they are not for every book. A wrap cover is an image that spans from the front of the book across the spine and around to the back of the book. If you hold the book up by its front and back covers there will be no break. This style is nice for several reasons. It prevents a boring back cover, it's usually less work for the designer since they only have to create one image and, most importantly, it makes the viewer want to see where the image goes so they flip the book over. This style is really great for dramatic books, children's books, and romance novels. Finance and business books, not so much - but even those can be done well. Do you have to do a wrap cover? No. Am I telling you all books should be a wrap cover? No. Do I want you to know what the heck the designer is talking about when they ask if you want a wrap cover? Yes.

TIP

If you do have a wrap cover or standard cover designed, have the designer give you the file with and without the text. The image might be just right for a poster or marketing.

What is PPI?

PPI is a term you hear often in publishing. It technically means Pixels Per Inch. The importance of getting the correct PPI cannot be stated enough. If you want an image to look clear in publishing you need to remember this: Most printed images need to be at 300 to be printed clearly in a book. Now online is another story; I will break it down for you.

1. For Print : Other than a few, and I do mean few exceptions, 300PPI is what you want for an image meant to go in or on a book.

2. For Web: When you move to an online format you need a few different options:

    a) Thumbnail : Thumbnail images are those little book cover you see online. They are tiny so they are an itsy bitsy 72PPI.

    b) Bookstore Online Images: Most bookstores will tell you that they also need a 150PPI image for larger display on their site....This is not the tiny image you see when doing a search. The image this refers to the one that is displayed if someone clicks on your book. It is the main information page on your title. The page will have your cover image, the books ISBN description, etc., as well as a buy button.

Rich Black

Rich Black is a topic near and dear to me because so few people make use of it. When you want a dark, beautiful black for your print book it is what you should use. Some printers will specifically ask for Rich Black. So what is it? Well it's just a color recipe you can use. **Black is not just black there are many shades of it and if you need the black to pop, you need to use this recipe:**

C: 60
M: 40
Y: 40
K: 100

TIP

If you are working in Photoshop, for a cover image or most Adobe products, go to: View>Proof setup>Working Black Plate

This will show you what the black looks like. If you are in CMYK, then type in the recipe above and make a mark. You should see the difference immediately!

RGB vs. CMYK

If you have been wondering what those little letters stand for this section is just what you need!

RGB: literally means Red Green and Blue. Your computer shows you things in RGB. A good rule of thumb is that if it is for the web or ebooks, RGB is your best bet.

CMYK: Cyan Magenta Yellow and Black (yep K is black) These are printer settings; when a book is printed, the actual printer uses a four color method that makes the colors truer to life and creates a more beautiful image. If you look at a CMYK image on a computer screen it is going to look goofy sometimes.

Remember:

Anything on a screen: RGB

Anything printed physically: CMYK

The Front Cover

- **Title:** Keep it short and sweet - not an overly long sentence.
- **Subtitle:** This is a place you can be more specific about a book. For example if you have a book on gardening titled *Container Gardening* then your subtitle might be: *What to plant and the best containers for it.*
- **Author name:** If you are using a real name or a pen name this is where it goes. Now unless you have a very popular series and are a known author, you want the title to be bigger than your name.
- **Other contributors:** If someone illustrated your book, or performed another important role, it goes on the cover as well.
- **Image :** Pick something eye catching but make sure it looks good thumbnail size for sales online.
- **Review quotes are some of the most powerful advertising you can do on your cover.** A person only has a moment or two to review the book before purchase, so a nice "best book of the year" or "A summertime must read!" is only going to help you. I will be going into reviews in more detail in the marketing book; but for cover purposes, if you have one, put it in a nice italic font and smack it on the top of your book. Make sure to put the source outside the quotation. If you have reviews but they are from people who are not in the industry, that is fantastic! Have them put their reviews on Amazon and Goodreads or Barnes and Noble - but keep off the cover. Reputable publications and sources are the only things that are cover worthy.
- **If your book is part of a series then you can also put the series name.** If you have a trilogy then you would want to write what number in the series your book is. For Example: *Book two of The Catacombs series.*

The Back Cover

Description: A good description is usually around 150 words, some are longer and some are shorter. For marketing, you are going to need three lengths 50, 150, and 300 word desriptions, but I will go into that more in the book *The Authors Guide to Surviving Self-publishing; Marketing.*

Other books published: If you have other books, put the name (or better yet, the cover images) small on the bottom.

Publisher logo: This can be simple and give a nice look.

Website: If you have a book or author site then list it here, you want fans to find you.

Bar-code: Many places supply these, so you may just need to leave room for it. Just check the template.

Author bio. and image: Are you an expert in your field or have other books out? There are a number of reasons to include an author bio. and photo on a book. Don't worry if you don't like pictures; you can just put the bio., people do it all the time.

TIP

When in doubt go to the library (libraries are great resources for self publishers.) and grab a book by an author you love and look at what they included on the back cover. Not sure what to look at? Find the New Release section and look at the titles for reference.

Files you need from your designer

You love your cover, it's fit to template and your dream of being a published author is nearly here. Before you part ways with your cover designer, there are a few things you need to make sure that you have:

Files:

- **Print Ready Cover File:** This is what you are actually giving to the printer or self-publishing platform. It needs to be fit to template, leave room for a bar-code and be in CMYK. Make sure it is the correct format of PDF and that there are no crop-marks or guides visible.

- **Front Cover for ebook:** This is a front cover only image in RGB (since it is meant for an ebook only). It must meet the requirements for the platform you are using. For example Amazon Kindle is:

"A minimum of 625 pixels on the shortest side and 1000 pixels on the longest side For best quality, your image should be 2500 pixels on the longest side"

What does that mean? Your designer will know but you should know how to check it. So if you open the file in Photoshop (since it's common to use this program, it's my example) along the top menu bar: IMAGE>Image size

Here's a screen-shot:

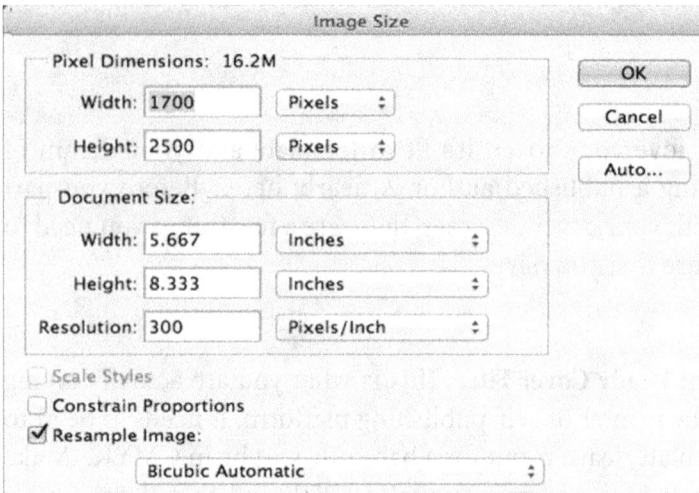

See where it says Pixel Dimensions? That is where you need it to be 2500 on the longest side.

- **Source file:** This is the most important file to get because it will allow any designer, or you, to make changes down the road. If the cover is done in Photoshop it will be a layered PSD file. If they are using InDesign have them package the file and zip it. These files are very big!!

- **Thumbnail:** A thumbnail size image is used on websites. It has 72 DPI and is in the RGB format.

- **3D book cover:** While not a necessity, is certainly is nice for marketing. Here is an example:

Publishing is evolving everyday so it is important to always put your best foot forward. A 3D cover can make your book standout. If you get one make sure you get it with a transparent background.

TO DO	✓	DATE DONE
ISBN assignent (one for each format)		
Select a printer or publishing service		
Get template		
Make sure images and fonts are ok to use commercially		
Get a Work For Hire Agreement		
Purchase a barcode if the book is going to be printed (not just digital) and you need to supply your own		
Interview designers, making sure they have the same timeframe you do		
Take notes and decide which designer is a good fit		
Get contact info		
Get all finished print ready and digital files		
• Print ready spread in CMYK		
• Front cover only for ebook (make sure it meets specs.)		
• Thumbnail size		
• 3D image for marketing if you can get it		
• Layered or packaged source file (save in two places so you don't lose it!)		

Use the following pages to review and select your designer, if you are planning to hire one. Take into account hourly rates vs. flat rate, revisions, and years in the business. Also make sure you have seen some of their work and that it's in-line with what you are imagining. You will also find a task list as well as a contact log. As you go through the publishing process it's important to know what steps you have done and those that need to be completed. You will meet and talk to many people along the way, if they are a good contact add them to your contact list. You may want to ask them for a review or a hand later.

5 QUESTIONS TO ASK YOUR DESIGNER BEFORE YOU HIRE THEM

1. What program do you use for cover layout?

Most professionals use Photoshop, InDesign or Illustrator.

2. How many revisions do you allow?

Make sure the designer allows for revisions until the book is ready to go to print. That being said, don't abuse or stress them with a million changes. Be respectful, keep the changes reasonable and remember: a full redesign after one is settled on is not a revision it's a redo.

3. Do you do the work yourself or do you subcontract it out?

You want to hire someone that is actually making your cover.

4. Do I need to purchase images?

Sometimes designers create images, use free images or belong to an imaging service. It's good to know up front if images will be an additional cost.

5. Will your provide me with the print ready cover spread as well as the source files?

Make sure they will give you the print ready files, fit to your template with all the elements you need, description etc. You also absolutely need the layered source file. You also want the front cover alone and sized to Kindle, this will take a good designer a few minutes and they shouldn't mind.

Use the follow pages as a tool for:

Hiring a designer
&
Keeping track of your publishing process

- **Questions for designers**
- **Questions for illustrators**
- **Questions for editors**
- **Contact log**
- **Publishing checklist**
- **Notes**

DESIGNER 1

Name: _____

Qualifications: _____

_____

_____

Did I like portfolio: Yes ☐ No ☐

Rate (fixed or hourly): _____

Years in industry: _____

Covers done: _____

Revisions allowed: _____

Program used: _____

Email: _____

Pros	Cons

References:

DESIGNER 2

Name: _____

Qualifications: _____

_____

_____

Did I like portfolio: Yes ☐ No ☐

Rate (fixed or hourly):_____

Years in industry: _____

Covers done: _____

Revisions allowed: _____

Program used: _____

Email: _____

Pros	Cons

References:

DESIGNER 3

Name: _____

Qualifications: _____

_____

_____

Did I like portfolio: Yes ☐   No ☐

Rate (fixed or hourly): _____

Years in industry: _____

Covers done: _____

Revisions allowed: _____

Program used: _____

Email: _____

Pros	Cons

References:

ILLUSTRATOR 1

Name: _____

Qualifications: _____

_____

_____

Did I like portfolio: Yes ☐ No ☐

Rate (fixed or hourly):_____

Years in industry: _____

Covers done: _____

Revisions allowed: _____

Program used: _____

Email: _____

Pros	Cons

References:

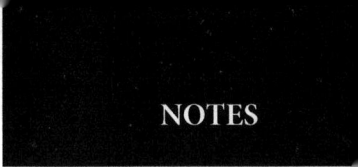

.

ILLUSTRATOR 2

Name: _____

Qualifications: _____

_____

_____

Did I like portfolio: Yes ☐   No ☐

Rate (fixed or hourly):_____

Years in industry: _____

Covers done: _____

Revisions allowed: _____

Program used: _____

Email: _____

Pros	Cons

References:

ILLUSTRATOR 3

Name: _____

Qualifications: _____

_____

_____

Did I like portfolio: Yes ☐ No ☐

Rate (fixed or hourly): _____

Years in industry: _____

Covers done: _____

Revisions allowed: _____

Program used: _____

Email: _____

Pros	Cons

References:

EDITOR 1

Name: _____

Qualifications: _____

_____

_____

Did I like portfolio: Yes ☐ No ☐

Is my book written in your
native language: Yes ☐   No ☐

Rate (fixed or hourly): _____

Years in industry: _____

Books done: _____

Revisions allowed: _____

Program used: _____

Email: _____

References:

Pros	Cons

References:

EDITOR 2

Name: _____

Qualifications: _____

_____

_____

Did I like portfolio: Yes ☐ No ☐

Is my book written in your
native language: Yes ☐ No ☐

Rate (fixed or hourly):_____

Years in industry: _____

Books done: _____

Revisions allowed: _____

Program used: _____

Email: _____

Pros	Cons

References:

EDITOR 3

Name: _____

Qualifications: _____

_____

_____

Did I like portfolio: Yes ☐ No ☐

Is my book written in your   Yes ☐ No ☐
native language: _____

Rate (fixed or hourly): _____

Years in industry: _____

Books done: _____

Revisions allowed: _____

Program used: _____

Email: _____

Pros	Cons

References:

Contact List (reviewers, authors, etc.)

	Name	Email or best way to contact

If you enjoyed this book please consider leaving it a review on Amazon, Goodreads and Barnes and Noble. Also check out some of the other titles that are out, or are coming out soon!

The Authors Guide to Surviving Self-publishing
Book Interiors

The Authors Guide to Surviving Self-publishing
CreateSpace

The Authors Guide to Surviving Self-publishing
Marketing

The Author's Guide to Surviving Self-publishing Book Interiors

There are many things that can make a book look self published and one of them is a low quality interior that does not meet industry standards. There are a few terms you are going to need to know for this and we will go through all of them in greater detail in their sections. If you come across something you already know then skip it, it's ok: this is a guide book not a novel. If you find an area that is very important then highlight it or even dog ear the page, I wont tell. The purpose is to have a short reference you can come back to time and again when you are getting your books ready for print. Now lets get to it.

Terms we will cover in this section:
Trim Size
Full Bleed
Gutter
Margins

In this first section we are going to start well before the layout itself even begins. Right after you finish writing and editing. Please take this one line and highlight it: **Do not start your layout until you have the final, edited text.** I cannot drive this point home enough. I have seen many occasions where a person will layout a book, it's beautiful and print ready and everyone is happy. Then the person will give the book to someone else who will make changes, sometimes big changes. The interior text gets altered and the layout has to be redone. This is a sticky situation for both you and your hopefully understanding designer. I am not telling you to put out a product that is less perfect in your eyes but I am telling you to prevent bad situations by being prepared and having everything all set before handing off to a designer.

Notes

Notes

The Authors Guide to Surviving Self Publishing: Covers

Notes

Notes

Notes

Notes

Notes

Notes

www.ingramcontent.com/pod-product-compliance
Lightning Source LLC
Chambersburg PA
CBHW060640280326
41933CB00012B/2099